HATE
AND
LOVE

J.L LEWIS

Gotham Books

30 N Gould St.
Ste. 20820, Sheridan, WY 82801
https://gothambooksinc.com/

Phone: 1 (307) 464-7800

© 2024 *J.L Lewis*. All rights reserved.

No part of this book may be reproduced, stored in a retrieval system, or transmitted by any means without the written permission of the author.

Published by Gotham Books (March 8, 2024)

ISBN: 979-8-88775-463-5 (H)
ISBN: 979-8-88775-461-1 (P)
ISBN: 979-8-88775-462-8 (E)

Because of the dynamic nature of the Internet, any web addresses or links contained in this book may have changed since publication and may no longer be valid.

The views expressed in this work are solely those of the author and do not necessarily reflect the views of the publisher, and the publisher hereby disclaims any responsibility for them.

TO THE EDITOR

In expressing an idea, one can be misunderstood. Without the proper use of words to convey an idea, the thought may be misrepresented to the hearer. I would like to bestow much thanks to Faith Lewis for her attention and keen ability to decipher what was written and present it within the context that I intended. Her ability to bring clarity to the ideas that are being expressed in this resource, and to sculpt them in a way that is palatable to the readers while maintaining their integrity and essence, is very much appreciated. Thank you for your humility and patience.

-J.L Lewis

CONTENTS

IDEA	1
THE IDEA VS. ANOTHER	5
THE FORMATION OF AN IDEA	8
WHAT IS THE NATURE OF A THING?	12
WHAT IS A SPIRIT?	20
WHAT IS A PERSON?	24
WHAT IS HUMAN?	30
THE FAMILY - המשפחה	48

INTRODUCTION

The Age of Enlightenment allowed for the emergence of the world as we know it. This era marked the cataclysmic shift to a society focused on and propelled by individual expression.

Discovering and accepting individualized identity is the quintessential factor that underpins the foundation and perpetuation of our new world order. This newfound identity is housed in the ability we possess to use our minds. The mindful journey of self-inquiry produced a wellspring of ideas, wherein, to be, is to be surrounded and taken by these ideas. We are joined to nations saturated with ideas, live in cities governed by them, and belong to communities that sometimes force them, albeit unwittingly, into our homes.

The home is where everything begins. It is a place designed for family; but now the ideas that we are engulfed by have reshaped the definition of what the home is, and who belongs to our family. Despite a wonderful emergence of new thought, something sinister was lying beneath the surface. The very ideas that we live by in our new world has created a wedge, an invisible barrier between the individual, and their natural home. This wedge will destabilize the individual, bringing us to a place where we no longer engage with ideas in a critical manner.

The fundamental tenets guiding our existence are quickly diminishing due to our neglect and dismissal of the axiomatic laws of thought. Our will is being suppressed and controlled by a way of thinking induced by destabilized individuals who form large and loud groups. We no longer see the causes to our effects, stifling the ability to reason into truth, and to properly exercise our hatred and love.

IDEA

All true ideas are contingent on reality, which is composed of time, space, matter, and energy. No pure idea is isolated in itself, nor can be dependent on itself. In conceptualizing the idea of a thought, one must know the person that the thought is related with for the idea to be contingent on reality. The statement here is reflecting how ideas come to be what they are. This is a result of the things we study and allow to dominate our thinking both consciously and subconsciously.

As written in Webster's Dictionary, an idea is a "formulated thought or opinion." Relayed by this, an idea is housed in all categories of behavior, which encompasses thought and actions that are related to rational beings.

Many of the great minds from the 18th and 19th centuries accepted the first verse of the Torah to be "The Idea of God (Elohim אלוהים)". This idea influenced thinkers like John Locke, who pioneered in establishing the main principles of the Enlightenment, which we now accept as core truths of reality and individuality. These truths, however far we have strayed from them, are contingent on this "Idea of God" written in the Bible. Truths such as an individual's potential, autonomy, and right to life are grounded in this verse.

"In the beginning, God created the heavens and the earth." Genesis 1:1 The first idea ever expressed *in itself* is found in the book of Ezekiel Chapter 28 verses 1-6 and 12-16.

"The word of the Lord came to me: "Son of man, say to the ruler of Tyre: This is what the Lord God says: Your heart is proud, and you have said, 'I am a god; I sit in the seat of gods in the heart of the sea."

Yet you are a man and not a god, though you have regarded your heart as that of a god. Yes, you are wiser than Daniel; no secret is hidden from you! By your wisdom and understanding you have acquired wealth for yourself. You have acquired gold and silver for your treasuries. By your great skill in trading, you have increased your wealth, but your heart has become proud because of your wealth." Therefore, this is what the Lord God says:"

"Son of man, lament for the king of Tyre and say to him: This is what the Lord God says: You were the seal of perfection, full of wisdom and perfect in beauty. You were in Eden, the garden of God. Every kind of precious stone covered you: carnelian, topaz, and diamond, beryl, onyx, and jasper, sapphire, turquoise and emerald. Your mountings and settings were crafted in gold; they were prepared on the day you were created. You were an anointed guardian cherub, for I had appointed you. You were on the holy mountain of God; you walked among the fiery stones. From the day you were created you were blameless in your ways until wickedness was found in you. Through the abundance of your trade, you were filled with violence, and you sinned. So, I expelled you in disgrace from the mountain of God, and banished you, guardian cherub, from among the fiery stones." (HCSB)

Other scriptures that accompany this are found in The Book of Isaiah Chapter 14 verses 12-22 and The Book of Revelations Chapter 12 verses 7-17.

The idea that is expressed by Lucifer (הילל "Helel") is not contingent on another, nor is the thought dependent on the words that were needed to form the correct structure of thought. Lucifer, being the brightest star that was ever created now exists as a being, viewing and understanding all that was needed to function as a living being. Lucifer, put his idea into words and not the words that cause(ed) all things to be. As stated at the beginning of this chapter, an idea is dependent on the other, and the other is not on the inside but on the outside.

In Genesis 1:1, The Creator created the heavens and the earth by and with The Word, sound, and breath. This is the Greatest Idea ever expressed, as the thoughts were being placed into words, by The Father. (Words are not necessarily dependent on sound and breath, however, sound and breath are necessary for words to be expressed.) The Word, which becomes the Son, Yeshua (ישוע) is being animated by The Holy Spirit who is responsible for the life and form of all things. In the first two verses of Genesis, there is no spoken word, no sound, only the formation of things. The word is being formed without breath. Just as the Holy Spirit is dependent on the Word for formation, and the Word is dependent on the Father for manifestation, it is clear that Each Person is dependent on the other, no one is doing, working, forming, or creating by themselves. The following scriptures offer a glimpse into the interconnected and dependent relationship that each person of the God-head has with one another. This dependency is etched in the blueprint of creation, and constantly carried out by created beings and things through their necessary contingencies.

Ezekiel 18:20 "The person who sins is the one who will die. A son won't suffer punishment for the father's iniquity, and a father won't suffer punishment for the son's iniquity. The righteousness of the righteous person will be on him, and the wickedness of the wicked person will be on him." (HCSB)

2 Corinthians 3:4-6 "We have this kind of confidence toward God through Christ. It is not that we are competent in ourselves to consider anything as coming from ourselves, but our competence is from God. He has made us competent to be ministers of a new covenant, not of the letter, but of the Spirit. For the letter kills, but the Spirit produces life." (HCSB)

John 5:7 "Sir," the sick man answered, "I don't have a man to put me into the pool when the water is stirred up, but while I'm coming, someone goes down ahead of me." (HCSB)

James 2:10-26 "For whoever keeps the entire law, yet fails in one point, is guilty of breaking it all. For He who said, Do not commit adultery, also said, Do not murder. So, if you do not commit adultery, but you do murder, you are a lawbreaker. Speak and act as those who will be judged by the law of freedom. For judgment is without mercy to the one who hasn't shown mercy. Mercy triumphs over judgment. What good is it, my brothers, if someone says he has faith but does not have works? Can his faith save him? If a brother or sister is without clothes and lacks daily food and one of you says to them, "Go in peace, keep warm, and eat well," but you don't give them what the body needs, what good is it? In the same way faith, if it doesn't have works, is dead by itself. But someone will say, "You have faith, and I have works." Show me your faith without works, and I will show you faith from my works. You believe that God is one; you do well. The demons also believe — and they shudder.

Foolish man! Are you willing to learn that faith without works is useless? Wasn't Abraham our father justified by works when he offered Isaac his son on the altar? You see that faith was active together with his works, and by works, faith was perfected. So, the Scripture was fulfilled that says, Abraham believed God, and it was credited to him for righteousness, and he was called God's friend. You see that a man is justified by works and not by faith alone. And in the same way, wasn't Rahab the prostitute also justified by works when she received the messengers and sent them out by a different route? For just as the body without the spirit is dead, so also faith without works is dead." (HCSB)

1 John 5:1 "Everyone who believes that Jesus is the Messiah has been born of God, and everyone who loves the Father also loves the one born of Him" (HCSB)

THE IDEA
VS. ANOTHER

The foundation of all things which must be observed in order to sustain lives, is the primary source. The Father gives the Word, and the Word creates all things, and the Spirit is forming and animating all things into what they will be. Lucifer did not rely on the primary principle that was set for functionality. He did not put reliance on the Word which the Creator designed for all living beings to function. Helel, rather, expressed an idea in himself that started, created, and caused a mixture of reality and imagination which then hindered him from the ability to distinguish between the two.

Lucifer said I will ascend to the heavens; I will set up my throne above the stars of God…I will ascend above the highest clouds; I will make myself like the Most High." Isaiah 14:13-14 (HCSB). What would prompt such a statement from this person, a being created perfectly in his purpose?

As Lucifer observed the dwelling place of YHWH in time, space, and matter, he was not able to locate YHWH (GOD) in time, space, and matter, so he said to himself, "I will be like God and sit in the seat of God". This idea is the beginning of the mixture of imagination and reality. The Creator is nontangible, non spatial, and non locational, so when Lucifer looked upon the dwelling place of God, he saw the throne, unoccupied. God in His essence has no relation to the created things as they are in creation, the only relationship that God has with the created things are with His Word. Yeshua (Jesus) was not yet seated at the right hand of the

Father in time, space, and matter. Lucifer thought to himself, in mixing reality with imagination, he can be like God (God does not function or act in accordance to design). The Word was already made and functioning in accordance to its design, however, not yet manifested in the flesh as a human person, Yeshua, or Jesus. The Word was only existing as the contingent form that we must rely on for ideas and operation. At this moment in time, in Helel's/Lucifer's mind, he said with all truthfulness from the outside and inside, that he will please the Creator, God, in a way he now designed, which is, to not function in accordance to his design. These ideas are repeated throughout time by mankind as we choose not to depend on the principles that were set by the Principle Giver, who continually show reliance on the other, rather than as individuals in themselves.

In Genesis 1:26, the events of the principle of dependence are recorded for mankind to see and follow. In the phrase "and God said (ויאמר אלהים)", the fullness of God is communicating with each person in the Godhead in time, space, energy, and matter. The Father is speaking the word as the Word is creating the thing, and the Holy Spirit is the one who animates the matter into living beings.

When we look closely at the word that is used for "creation", and the word which is used to create 'the Adam', it is the same word "bara (ברא)". This Hebrew word "bara" shows forth the principle clearly. Nothing comes from nothing and all things that came into being are dependent on the same things. That thing must possess the building blocks (the word that all creation is contingent on) for its meaning to be apprehended in reality.

The Adam is dependent on the basic elements of all created things. The water, which has an atomic value of one, the air which has an atomic value of eight, the earth which has an atomic value of seven, and fire which has an atomic value of six. Each of these elements, when combined, the resulting atomic value is a very unique number. The water, which is the liquid, is hydrogen (1). The air, which is the gas, is oxygen (8). The earth, which is solid, is nitrogen (7). The fire, which is the combustion, is carbon, (6). They all total the number 22. The number twenty-two is the total amount of numbers that formed the Hebrew Alphabet. The Hebrew letters are thought by the sages to be the very things which are responsible for Creation of the physical world.

The Adam is dependent on matter, and matter (space, time, and energy) is dependent on the word, which are the letters of the Hebrew alphabet, the oot- אות or ooteoth- אותות. The word is an intangible thing, and the matter, space, time, and energy is a tangible materials; each dependent on the other to be what they are in reality.

THE FORMATION
OF AN IDEA

When we look at Elohim and Lucifer/Helel, we tend to think that one opposes the other. As we now understand, Lucifer was created, and Elohim is. As a result of creation, right and wrong, good and bad, truth vs. falsehood, up and down, love and hate, all came to be what they are and are contingent on, yet opposed to the other.

Let us take a closer look and see how the idea of sin, dysfunctionality, evil, and wickedness was formed. In the book of Ezekiel chapter 28 verse 15, YHWH said to Helel, "You were blameless in your ways, from the day you were created until wrongdoing was found in you". We will look at the word "found - עד-נמצא ead-ne-mee-tsaah", the word "מצא" matsa" is conjugated with another word, "עד-ead" and "נ-nun".

The word matsa in its infinitive form, means to find deliberately or bring out. The "nun-נ" means new life springing out, bud. The "אד-ead" means eternity, until witness. The next word, "wrongdoing - עולל -oolel" has the meaning, baby, infant, perpetrate, commit, do evil, misuse power. Lucifer, being a contingent being, now brings into existence an idea that has no reliance on the created word which ought to support all ideas in their conception. Lucifer now gives birth to dysfunctionality.

All things were created, that includes Yeshua (The Word), Lucifer, angels, and physical persons. All personable beings were created to function and depend on that which is necessary for their existence, which is the spoken word. A person is one that has a mind, will, intellect, intelligence, and emotions.

Lucifer, a created person in time, space, matter, and energy, birthed into reality his imagination. Being the seal of perfection, full of wisdom, perfect in beauty, and in the mountain of Elohim, he mixed his thought(s) with the reality he was exposed to. Lucifer, a contingent being, decided in himself that he will not function according to his design, but will please Elohim, YHWH, by being like Him, nonfunctional.

As a result of the mixture of imagination with reality by Lucifer/Helel, all created beings, visible and invisible, now stand the possibility of being influenced by their imagination. We who are visible created beings, when using the terms, good and bad, right and wrong, truth vs. falsehood, love and hate, what are we referring to? Is it the flesh, the mind, or the things that are created? In Genesis 1:31 "God saw all that He had made and found it very good." Until this point in time, there was no kind of visible dysfunctionality, or thing that can be created as evil, bad, or wicked. The angels and heavenly hosts were already in existence as the physical, visible universe was being created. Things are made to function in accordance with design. All what Elohim had made was Good in His Word. We are seeing in Ezekiel 28, the emergence of the idea that is isolated in itself, which is a contradiction because it reflects and depends only on itself, therefore it is only an opinion. This results in sin, evil, wickedness, or dysfunction.

John 8:44 "You are of your father the devil and you want to carry out your father's desires. He was a murderer from the beginning and has not stood in the truth, because there is no truth in him. When he tells a lie he speaks from his own nature, because he is a liar and the father of liars."

As we just read, sin, or evil, is not a thing, but a person by maturity. That person is Helel/Lucifer, whose name changed to Satan. In the transformation of Lucifer to Satan, we see the imagination of a person being mixed with the created, trying to make it reality, bringing about a non relational separation, which is death.

In the pattern of Helel's/Lucifer's non relational separation, we as created persons see what not to mix: desire and imagination. However, that pattern was accepted by Adam, and they ended up with the same fate as Lucifer, a non relational separation.

When reality and imagination are mixed together with visible created persons who are not actualized, the ability to discern between truth, error, love, hate, right, wrong, matter, energy, light, waves, sounds, vibrations, particles, quarks, anything, is impaired.

In the fall of 'the Adam', the created world was affected, and the idea of Creation needed to be reinforced with the living word or, manifested word, Yeshua, as a human being. In Lucifer's fall, he did not depend on the literal Word. As he imagined in his mind, he mixed his ideas with himself, an invisible created being, and thereby, became the Creator of the thing we call sin.

All the things that make him what he is now supports his idea on another word, which is his opinion being spoken out to his Creator, Yahweh. God said to Lucifer, "Why is iniquity found in your heart?". That which is now knowable by Lucifer, is supported by and with the thing that has been created to function as a part necessary for the whole. Once being the anointed cherub who covers, he functioned as part of a unit. Being confronted with God's question, Lucifer affirms his own idea, this new whole, that is contingent on a part, which is himself. This new whole is separated from the prior functioning part of the unit. Lucifer is now isolated in himself as a part, which was his created identity, and a whole, his new idea. The part that is not dependent on the whole of creation, but on the part of creation, which is himself, now becomes a whole in himself, who is Satan. He now exists as an adversary to the created realm. This is the beginning of dysfunctionality, sin, wickedness, evil, and all the words that relate with those ideas; the incipience of the statement, "Be true to thyself". Now lies the confusion of up, down, right, left, front, back, hot, cold, black, white, etc, due to the mixture of imagination and desire. The observation of reality becomes harder to distinguish from imagination. Truth becomes indistinguishable from falsehood, and love from hate. As clearly stated by James, the brother of Jesus, a person, when consumed by their imagination, makes unnatural room for their desires, giving birth to a new aspect of reality that is void of life.

James 1:14-15 But each person is tempted when he is drawn away and enticed by his own evil desires. Then after desire has conceived, it gives birth to sin, and when sin is fully grown, it gives birth to death. (HCSB).

WHAT IS THE NATURE OF A THING?

What is a thing? We as a people are used to the word thing. We use expressions like, "Look at that thing", "Do you remember that thing I was telling you about?" Or "I know that thing that you are talking about, but I can't remember its name." Things are all around us whether we know them by their name or not, they are there.

Merriam-Webster dictionary defines a thing as "1: an object or entity not precisely designated or capable of being designated 2 a: an inanimate object distinguished from a living being, b: a separate and distinct individual quality, fact, idea, or usually entity, c: the concrete entity as distinguished from its appearances, d: a spatial entity."

To ask the question, "What is a thing?" there must be a contingent element existing in order to voice the question. Upon voicing the question to others, or to oneself, it requires a response from another. We should never rely on ourselves for the answer because of the uncertainties of our thoughts and biases. However, due to the decline of critical thinking in many aspects of society, we unfortunately do rely on ourselves for answers. People want to live in their truth while sacrificing The Truth that corresponds with all reality. To explore this objective Truth, and to find the meaning of any thing we must look into books, nature, and similar images and thoughts that correspond to the question that is being asked.

A material object must exist in order for things to be what they are. Only the material object can disclose and reveal what that thing is. As we saw in the definition, it goes from a tangible to a nontangible thing, and at all times, remains physical.

The way we view things today is as a result of the evolution of the word "thing". The word "ping" from Old English meant, meeting, assemble, council, discussion. Then it later changed to mean entity, being, matter (subject of deliberation in an assembly), act, deed, event, material object, body, being, creature. Today, it is material objects and thoughts. As a result of material and thought, two main lines of philosophy emerge: spiritual (invisible), and physical (visible). Plato said all that exists are forms, and Aristotle says all is matter. These early Greek philosophers split the physical world into two: the tangible-visible, and intangible-invisible, thus, creating a dichotomy of the physical creation which is both seen and unseen. The spiritual and physical are blurred with the non-temporal, non-physical, non-tangible, necessary being, Yahweh. The absence of a thing does not necessarily mean the absence of a person.

The understanding of the word "thing" brings a sense of uncertainty with reality. If a thing is not clearly defined, then reality as it is, cannot be known, and maybe, we are just molecules in motion, as stated by some atheists. We cannot redefine a thing based upon our ignorance, or our refusal to accept the information that has been made known through the thing itself, or by another who created that thing.

To dispel the past and present ideas of what a thing is, we must go back to the etymological derivation of the prima lingua. We must go back to the origin of all things.

The Bible is a familiar book, with which we are all hopefully aware of. In the book of Genesis (Old Testament) and The Gospel of John (New Testament), the first chapter and first verse, tells us how all things came into existence. The book of Genesis speaks of beginnings and tells us how all things began. In order for this understanding of things to be grasped, we have to go back to the Hebrew language, which caused all things to be what they are.

The book opens with a word, Barasheet, בראשית. In Hebrew, each letter is a word, and the word itself consists of the number of letters that are other individual words. The word barasheet has six words all combined together that form one word, which is translated in the King James Version of the Bible as "In the Beginning".

The first letter, or word, is a house בית - bayit, which is the meaning of the letter "ב". A deeper meaning of this letter is distinction, two, inside, outside, and separation. The dichotomy the philosophers came to during the classical period in Ancient Greece, came directly from the second letter of the Hebrew Alphabet.

The bet is the letter that discloses all reality as it distinguishes between inside, outside, up, down, right, left, physical, spiritual, love, and hate. This letter reveals the reality of all created things, as the tangible and intangible are one and the same. One cannot be separated from the other in its essence. The physical appears to conceal the spiritual. We can only know the information of a thing through what is revealed. Apart from that thing, we cannot know anything about that thing. The bet is the house that represents the universe and all that is contained in it. As stated in Hugh Ross's book "Why the Universe Is the Way It Is",

> "Anyone who hasn't had the privilege of studying astrophysics may not realize that the universe must be as massive as it is, or human life would not be possible - for at least two reasons. The first concerns the production of life-essential elements. The density of protons and neutrons in the universe relates to the cosmic mass, or mass density. That density determines how much hydrogen, the lightest of the elements, fused into heavier elements during the first few minutes of cosmic existence. And the amount of heavier elements determines how much additional heavy-elements production occurs later in the nuclear furnaces of stars. If the density of protons and neutrons were significantly lower (than enough to convert about 1 percent of the universe's mass into stars), then nuclear fusion would proceed less efficiently. As a result, the cosmos would never be capable of generating elements heavier than helium - elements like carbon, nitrogen, oxygen, phosphorus, sodium, and potassium, which are

essential for any kind of physical life. On the other hand, if the density of protons and neutrons were slightly higher (enough to convert significantly more than 1 percent of the mass of the universe into stars), nuclear fusion would be too productive. All the hydrogen in the universe would rapidly fuse into elements as heavy as, or heavier than, iron. Again, essential elements (carbon, nitrogen, oxygen, etc), including hydrogen, would not exist."

The finely tuned nature of our large universe is what allows the elements responsible for sustenance and life to exist.

Just as the universe is contingent on the basic elements for its existence, in the same way, all of creation is contingent on the bet. As the universe contains the elements for life, it reflects the basic function of a house. All that is needed for reproduction, fruitfulness, and security, are found therein.

The bet ב is the second letter in the structure of the aleph-bet which has a numerical value of two and is at the right hand of the Aleph - א. The Aleph just happens to be the first letter of the Aleph-bet. The way in which the Torah has been structured by Ruach HaKodesh (The Holy Spirit), the letters give hints and clues about the Persons of God. The clues, or hints, come from a Hebrew acronym, referred to as Pardes (PRDS), a word meaning "orchard" consisting of four approaches to interpretation midrashically. As expressed by James Jacob Prasch in "Shadows of the Beast".

> The "P" represents "Peshat"- the simple, straightforward meaning.
>
> The "R" represents "Remes"- meaning "clues" or "hint".
>
> The "D" represents "Drash" - meaning "homiletical application"
>
> The "S" represents "Sod" - meaning "a secret meaning" that in certain contexts, relates to a possible Pesher interpretation.

As the scripture culminates in the New Testament, the person of the Bet/Bayit-House, The Savior, is revealed in various portions of writings.

Acts 7:56 "Look! I see the heavens opened and the Son of Man standing at the right hand of God".

Romans 8:34 "Who is the one who condemns? Christ Jesus is the One who died, but even more, has been raised; He also is at the right hand of God and intercedes for us."

Ephesians 1:20 "He demonstrates this power in the Messiah by raising Him from the dead and seating Him at His right hand in the heavens."

Colossians 3:1 "So if you have been raised with the Messiah, seek what is above, where the Messiah is, seated at the right hand of God."

Hebrews 1:3 "He is the radiance of His glory, the exact expression of His nature, and He sustains all things by His powerful word. After making purification for sins, He sat down at the right hand of the majesty on high."

The "Bet" represents the son, the second person of the Godhead. The bet is showing the contingency on the "Aleph", which is to the left of the "Bet".

When the term Messiah or "Christ Jesus" is used to speak about Jesus, who is mankind's saviour, it is referring to His Divine Nature as God the Son who is coming again as a judge. The son is separated, selected to love dutifully, to give what belongs to the other. In the beginning of The Gospel according to John, the author says, "In the beginning was the Word and the Word was with God and the Word was God." As we are seeing, the bet hints to us, it represents God in time, space, and matter, as a thing, a Person. That thing, which is now physical, can only be made within the thing that has been made visible, which is the Word, who is the person, Yeshua.

The Hebrew word for "thing" is Daber, דבר, which means to "combine separate items into one"[1]. A thing is both physical and spiritual. Letters and numbers are reminiscent of this. One can see a letter; however, the number is discovered through the observance and study of that letter. You cannot have a letter without a number, the same way you cannot have the physical without the spiritual and vice versa. Reality requires that distinction to be made in order for things to be what they are. You cannot have one without the other.

The word "daber" is also translated as "word", so the letter is a thing, and the thing is a word; the word is responsible for the creation of all things. Psalm 33:6 Isaiah 42:5 Psalms 136:5 John 1:3 Colossians 1:16.

Now, some reading may be a bit confused at the statement just made, "the spiritual and physical are the same", some may not. The statement may appear to affirm pantheism, panentheism, and many other monistic religions. When I say spirit or spiritual, I am referring to that which is not seen, heard, or felt, by and with our natural senses. These things, however, can be observed with specifically designed machines and techniques performed by diviners.

We can now view the function of particles under a microscope, with this, we have discovered the vast amount of information that is housed within. With the field of quantum mechanics, and the famous double-slit experiment, we see the probable and interchangeable nature of things. Light and matter act as both waves and particles depending on the circumstances. This probable nature of energy and matter exemplifies the enigmatic nature of reality, the spiritual and physical. This is where science has reached thus far.

Science always questions the unknown, or the indescribable. That which is unexplainable now, will be explained at the appointed time. This is stated by Paul in 2 Corinthians 12:2-4. Science can only carry you to a certain point into the unknown and unexplainable, but the Holy Spirit is

---

[1] Matityahu Clark, Samuel Raphael Hirsch, Etymological Dictionary of Biblical Hebrew: Based on the Commentaries of Rabbi Samson Raphael Hirsch (Jerusalem, Israel: Feldheim Publishers, 1999), 46.

who makes the unknowable known. Information can be viewed as the spirit, however without the substance, the spirit or information cannot be known.

God הוה׳- Yahweh, is not a thing, nor can he exist or become. Things became what they are. The letter 'bet' became a word, and that word was a thing as it came into being in time, space, matter, and energy, all at once.

God as the Son, the bet ב, became (in time, space, matter, and energy), forming the universe. After God the Father formed the Universe by His Word, we see the bet to be more than just a letter. The bet becomes the first person ever created, and the person who is responsible for the beginning of time, space, matter, and energy, which we know as information or spirit.

Information and knowledge, when used skillfully, are known to many as wisdom. Wisdom is the understanding of knowledge and the skillful use of information at any given time.

We see in Proverbs 8:22-36, before anything was made or created, the "thing" wisdom was there: "The Lord made me at the beginning of His creation before His works of long ago. I was formed before ancient times from the beginning before the earth began. I was born when there were no watery depths and no springs filled with water. I was delivered before the mountains and hills were established, before He made the land, the fields, or the first soil on the earth. I was there when He established the heavens, when He laid out the horizon on the surface of the ocean, when He placed the skies above, when the fountains of the ocean gushed out, when He set a limit for the sea so that the waters would not violate his command, when He laid out the foundations of the earth. I was a skilled craftsman beside Him. I was His delight every day, always rejoicing before Him. I was rejoicing in His inhabited world, delighting in the human race, and now, my sons, listen to me; those who keep my ways are happy. Listen to instruction and be wise; don't ignore it. Anyone who listens to me is happy, watching at my doors everyday, waiting by the posts of my doorway. For the one who finds me finds life and obtains favor from the Lord, but the one who misses me harms himself; all who hate me love death."

The "Word"- דבר is called wisdom - chochmah חכם, which means to accumulate knowledge. (Ibid pg. 80) We all know in our world there are two types of wisdom, earthly wisdom, and heavenly wisdom. In our culture, when a person possesses a certain amount of knowledge, he is thought to be wiser, or more spiritual than others. As the saying goes, the one who knows more wins, or so to speak.

The thing we hold on to will determine our destiny, and as stated, the thing is the information or spirit we hold on to as the Truth. The only way to understand anything or information that exists, the person that created all things must speak. Genesis 1:3 is the first time the "bet" spoke, who is the son: "And Elohim said" - "ויאמר אלהים". The word aamear - אמר, when translated in the Bible is the word "said". The root meaning is "organized speech to be heard and understood", (ibid pg 12) by all intelligent beings.

Intelligence must exist in order to know a thing, and the thing that begins to exist must be intelligent in order to be known in itself and by others.

So, what is a thing? A thing is the letter or the word that was created by the Creator, and has the information of itself in itself, which is the word of God that was given to man as organized speech, known as "The Torah". Stated another way; a thing is that which is given by the Father, unknown in its essence, however, knowable through the information of creation and the divine revelation of the Holy Scriptures.

WHAT IS A SPIRIT?

As stated by Dictionary.com, a spirit is "the principle of conscious life; the vital principle in humans, animating the body or mediating between body and soul. The incorporeal part of humans." A spirit is also defined as a conscious, incorporeal being, as opposed to matter.

The Greek word for spirit is 'Pneuma' and can sometimes be referred to in a way which emphasizes one's personality and character. The word, as used in the middle of the thirteenth century, means animating, or vital principle in man and animals; spirit/soul. In Latin, 'spiritus', means breathing, respiration, and the wind, breath of God, breath of life, vigor, courage, pride, arrogance, or to blow.

We must clarify between the different types of spirits that have been revealed in scripture, and the spirits that have been observed by the men of old. There are three types of relational spirits revealed to humans: the human, angelic, and divine spirit.

As we have stated before, a thing gives information of itself. Now, we will show a spirit that begins to exist, has a direct relation with its creator and its state of being. The Bible reveals three types of spirits: the divine spirit who is the Holy Spirit, the third person of The Elohim, has no beginning, was not made, and is only known through The Word; the angelic spirits, who were made before the visible universe and galaxies; and lastly, we have the human spirit, which is the spirit we will be looking at as we view the nature of "the Adam".

Humans, "man Adam-אדם", are known to be composed of matter, mind, and spirit/soul. From the moment of conception, the person of a human begins. In the case of Jesus, the beginning of a thing as part of visible reality, becoming flesh and blood, does not negate the personhood of that thing, which is The Eternal Word of Elohim. Through the investigation of the Hebrew scriptures, we see the person of Christ manifested in the being of Yeshua. We humans know what we are by observing the essence of our beings. We are matter by nature, visible. We are intellectual, which allows us to be intelligent. We each have the ability to reason, and then carry out the will of our intellect, which is then demonstrated in our feelings and emotions, and finally, brings about the right of choice, to choose between, right and wrong, love or hate, truth or falsehood. This is how we know we are spirit, we are independent yet dependent. We can only know of a spirit through the thing that has been made. We know that we possess a spirit through the information that has been given universally, then realized individually in our physical bodies, and revealed in the Holy Scriptures: The Tanakh and The New Testament.

The ability to relate with visible and nonvisible information, within oneself, and outside of oneself, is the quintessential state of independence. This independence of thought is what classifies the spirit of a person. We see a differentiation of physical and spiritual in the scripture, Romans 7:25 "I thank God through Jesus Christ our Lord! So then, with my mind I myself am a slave to the law of God, but with my flesh, to the law of sin."

A spirit is a person who has all the necessary information of oneself and possesses the ability to distinguish between the many opposites that are presented to them. This person now can see inside and outside, and choose between love, hate, right, wrong, truth, or falsehood. They are distinct while also making distinctions.

A spirit should only follow the information that was placed in that person. How do we know this? The Hebrew word "ruach - רוח" is translated in Genesis 1:2 as "wind". The child root רוח-ruach comes from the parent root רח-rach, while this root is not found in the biblical text, several other words derived from its root. The word "ארח - arah" means "to travel", "ירח - yareach" is "the moon", and "רחה - recheh" is "a millstone". What does wind, traveling, moon, and millstone all have in common? They each have to do with following a prescribed path. The wind follows the same path each season, a traveler follows a path, the moon follows the same path in the sky and a millstone also follows a "prescribed path". (The Living Words page 72, Jeff Benner)

The spirit of man also has a prescribed path to follow, The Word. Exemplifying scriptures are found in The Gospel according to John 5:19, 4:24, 6:63 and Psalm 119:105-112. "Your word is a lamp to my feet and a light to my path."

The spirit of man can no longer follow the Spirit of the Father as they were designed to. Due to the fall of humankind, the spirit of man was contaminated and can no longer identify the Truth, what is right and good, in its essence. The spirit of man now needs another spirit of the same kind, to reestablish the relationship that man had with the Father in the garden. The spirit that was given is the Holy Spirit after the sacrifice of the flesh of Yeshua and the spilling of His blood for the reconciliation of all mankind. The Holy Spirit can now enter the man's spirit through the preaching of the physical Yeshua, who fulfilled the Tanach, together with the written word that corresponds to His life lived ministry.

The human spirit is information, and the divine spirit is The Word (Old and New Testament), while the angelic spirit is what scripture says they are. Things make information known; however, the absence of a thing does not negate the presence of information. The things that make information possible are intelligence, speech, signs, and codes.

An excerpt from a scientific article titled "Biological Information - What is it" by Werner Gitt, Robert Crompton, and Jorge Fernandez, gives a clear rendition of exactly how information and what we are exploring as "spirit" are truly connected.

"Dr Gitt (et al.), a world-recognized specialist in information theory, provides an overview of *functional information*. Dr Gitt et al. show that biological information is exactly the same type of information that we use every day in our electronic communications. Biological information is what makes life alive, in the same way information gives life to our computers, the internet, and modern society. Like any type of real-world information, biological information entails language (symbolic representation and grammar), meaning (an informative message or specification), and purpose (an expected result). Dr. Gitt et al. show that information is itself a *non-material entity* - it is neither matter nor energy. Mere matter cannot create information or information systems."

Jesus said in

John 14:6 "I am the way, the truth, and the life. No one comes to the Father except through Me."

The Hebrew meaning of the words: way, truth, and life, give information from the Divine, Yahweh Elohim.

Way - דרך - step forward, progress toward a goal.

Truth - אמת - to see things for what it is, from the front, middle, and back. Clear.

Life - חיה - live by virtue of God's thoughts.

John 4:24 "God is a Spirit, and those who worship Him must worship Him in spirit and truth." We as men are to live a life in the spirit, and the Hebrew is giving us a clear meaning of what that looks like!

Men are to step forward when they hear the Word of God, and press toward the goal of the Truth which is to see things for what they are, clearly. This allows us to live by the virtue of God's thoughts, which is the wholeness of a man who now worships God in spirit and truth.

WHAT IS A PERSON?

According to Dictionary.com, a person is "a human being, whether an adult or child" and "a human being as distinguished from an animal or a thing." A person is a being that has the capability to reason, exercise morality, and possess consciousness along with self-consciousness.

From the beginning of the thirteenth century A.D., the word person was used to describe a human, and as we are all familiar with the way we choose to define a thing, it is in that way we relate with that thing. As the word person is used to relate with a human, a human was then and is now related to as a person.

When we hear the question "What is a Person?" the first response we give is a human being. For the average mind, a person is a human being, and personhood never goes beyond the human being or mind. A human being is a person; however, a person is not limited to a human being.

Genesis 1:26 "And God said let us make man in our image, after our likeness" "ויאמר אלוהים נעשה אדם בצלמנו כדמותנו"

The material that The Creator is using to make the man, who is a person, is the same material that was used to create the universe. The word "amar" which is translated as "said", is revealing a clear understanding of how we know what a thing is, and what the difference is between things that were made, and the thing, Adam, that is now being made. This is why astrophysicists and other scientists can say we are just stardust, all material.

They can say that, and it is evident in the findings of the observable things. All material things have one common thread. This conclusion can be reached because of the organized structure and the understanding of each separate thing by these scientists. The things being observed did not come about through evolution.

How did all of these scientists come to one true conclusion? The reason is, they can observe, understand, and relate to the universe and all the physical things that are observable in it. Furthermore, it is because of the meaning of the word, "amar". The word amar means "organized speech to be heard and understood". ²

All animals and other living things are able to understand their purpose and objective and carry them out in accordance with their design. Every day the universe shows that it is operating by certain laws, functioning in accordance with its design specifications. All of this is knowable because of the word amar אמר.

The man did not become a person when the Creator Elohim spoke, as He spoke all other things into existence. However, the man only became a person when Yahweh Elohim formed the Adam from the dust of the Earth. He blew into his nostrils the breath of life, and man became a living being.

The man who is now alive is not like the other animals that were made by Elohim's command, nor like the angels that were made before the visible, solid, universe. The Adam is uniquely made in the image of Yahweh צלם יהוה אלוהים.

In Genesis 1:26, Elohim said, "let us make mankind in our image after our likeness." In this verse, the plurality of the Creator is being made known to Adam. The three persons, Father, Son, and Holy Spirit are all operating as One, while the Adam observes the physical relationship with the Word and the universe.

---

² Matityahu Clark, Samuel Raphael Hirsch, Etymological Dictionary of Biblical Hebrew: Based on the Commentaries of Rabbi Samson Raphael Hirsch (Jerusalem, Israel: Feldheim Publishers, 1999), 12.

In Genesis 2:7, the plurality of the Creator presents themselves as individuals in the formation of the one, Adam, from the dust of the Earth. The Father is revealed as Yahweh - יהוה, the Son as Elohim - אלוהים, and the Spirit, יפה - breath. Each one of these things, "words", that are revealed, cannot be known in isolation. Each one is contingent on the other, necessary for the others to be known.

The Adam is a physical representative of the three persons that are necessary for Creation, and a physical representation of the personhood of the Creator. The Woman is taken out of the Man, and the Child is a whole person, as a result of the Man and Woman becoming one in copulation. The Child is now made as the Creator is in time, dependent on another. The Child, as we observed, possesses a mind, intellect, intelligence, will, emotions, and feelings. From observing the Adam and finding what and who we are, we can know what and who the Creator is.

The single individual, Adam - אדם, was made, and out of that unit the Creator brought forth another of the same essence, different in function and operation, called the Woman. The Adam who was made one, became two, man and woman; they are of the same kind and essence but different in function and sex. The Adam becoming two and being a representative of the Creator does not necessitate the Creator possessing sex. This is a distinguishment of the Creator from the Creation.

The inanimate object, the earth/dust was not made into a living being or person, until the neshama - נשמה (breath) of Elohim Yahweh was placed into the earth - adamah - אדמה, who now possesses the tsalem - צלם (image) of God. The Adam coming into being, was not made like the other animals. Genesis 2:19 says, "So the LORD God formed out of the ground every wild animal and every bird of the sky and brought each to the man to see what he would call it." Genesis 2:20:b "but for the man no helper (eazor - עזר) was found who was like (kenegdo - כנגדו) him."

Before the woman was brought to the man, he was sent to the animals. The Adam can relate with, communicate with, and talk with the animals. He can be and do all things that are instinctively possible with the animals. One thing he could not do is become one with the animals. He could not relate with any animal as a person. The animals did not have the tsalem neshemah of Yahweh Elohim.

We are now seeing the nature of man that is different from the nature of animals. The man is using his soul/spirit to identify likeness in accordance with rationality rather than instinctiveness. The man before the fall had the information within himself (uncorrupted from the outside) of his purpose.

The relationship that the Adam must have must come from the inside, from the One. In this development we see that relationship only comes from its cause, and this relationship is rational, logical, and reasonable. At this time, the woman person was presented to the man, and he said, "This one at last is bone of my bone and flesh of my flesh. This one shall be called woman." Genesis 2:23. The need for relationship is the willingness to die and give what belongs to the other willingly. This is seen in the sleep of the man, as the woman was taken out of him, and in the birth of a child as it is released from the mother; always giving what is not yours willingly. This pattern is seen in the Father Yahweh giving the Son Yahshua, and the Son giving the Spirit. Each person is from the Elohim, and at the same time, are the Elohim; one essence, three different persons.

How do we know that we are Persons? This is how we know: the spiritual existence cannot be known apart from the physical existence. The physical sets the boundaries of our freedom, which all intelligent beings have in order to function. Freedom is the visible and invisible lines that are set for intelligent beings' continual existence with the Creator Elohim. The spiritual, or information, is then known through the boundaries/freedom of the physical. As was stated in chapter one, the information can be referred to as the Spirit, who gives direction to The Way, The Truth, and The Life. John 14:6 Romans 1:20, 2:14-15.

Man has a very distinct resemblance to the Creator Elohim, and that is seen in his intellect. Not all intelligent beings are rational and only rational beings can choose Yeshua. Joshua 1:8 Daniel 11:32 Matthew 7:22-23. The book of Hosea chapter 4:6 states "My people are destroyed for lack of knowledge. Because you have rejected knowledge, I will reject you from serving as My priest. Since you have forgotten the law of your God, I will also forget your sons." Without information and knowledge, we cannot know of anything that is physical or spiritual. The Spirit or information of the spiritual and consciousness is bringing us back to the physical information, and at the same time, the physical points us to the invisible and spiritual information.

Information is bound to its created state, as it can only be known or understood in Creation. Information is limited to all contingent beings, visible and invisible. The Apostle Paul said in 1 Corinthians 13:12 and 2 Corinthians 12:2 We know in part and there are things which cannot be known. We can know the outcome of information, which is the knowledge of the thing, however, the information itself cannot be known in its exclusivity. We can know and recognize the information for what is expressed or revealed, at the same time, the information that is revealed can only be known through the thing that has been revealed to the degree of the seeker's search.

Charles Darwin postulated that the cell is just a formless blob of protoplasm. Darwin was only exposed to the limited information and spirit of his day. As we know today, there are numerous parts that make up the cell: the protein, RNA, and DNA, to name a few.

The Hebrew word for information is Medah - מידע, and it comes from a Hebrew root Yadah - ידע, which means "acquire knowledge, know".[3] This is what the spirit is, knowledge and information.

The Spirit is the hand that opens or closes the door of your mind's eyes to the things in this world. This is man's spirit, or all created, intelligent, spirits. Man's spirit is like Yahweh Elohim's spirit in the sense of information. Information is as a result of creation or created things. Information was never made or began to exist; it was only known after an invisible and visible mind was created. The spirit is not limited to things and can only be known as spirit or information as the physical mind is observed.

The information, understanding, and wisdom of a mind, visible and invisible, can only be fully known through the person who made all things, Yeshua Ha'Mashiach, Jesus the Christ. Proverbs 8:22-36 and 2 Thessalonians 2:1-17.

WHAT IS HUMAN?

As stated by Dictionary.com, a human is, of, relating to, or characteristic of, humans. The idea of people or humans was recorded by Protagoras of Abdera around 400 BC as he viewed society's values.

As stated in *Great Thinkers of the Western World* by Ian P. McGreal "Protagoras was particularly attentive to the value of social life. He represented the typical Greek view that no one is absolutely self-sufficient; all are members of a society, the existence of which is in itself a great gift from the gods. In the Platonic dialogue the *Protagoras*, Plato has the first Sophist articulate what scholars refer to as the Protagoras myth regarding the beginnings of things. The focus of his speech is on the question of what is necessary for survival." Here is where he uses the gods to console the behavior of the people changing the classification of persons to humans. "The gods, he tells us, have offered to some animals strength to defend themselves; to others, smallness, so that they can escape, while to birds the ability to fly is given. The gods ordained that some animals would feed upon others, while all species together would form a *cosmos*, a well balanced order. Turning to mankind, the gods remained attentive to the problem of their survival. To this end, they offered to humanity two great gifts; first, fire—in broad terms, technical power over nature....Thus, Zeus, fearing that their race would utterly perish, offered to human beings the social impulse that binds them and the whole of civilization. This is the greatest gift offered to humanity, the gift of social community, the bonds of social interrelationship that give rise to feelings of solidarity with other human beings" (McGreal 13).

Protagoras can be seen as the father of the human race, which is expressed in communities. These communities, although they have different roles of individuals, work together for the good of the whole. This was viewed as virtuous, a trait of excellence in the human that begins to operate within their community.

Present ideals in our universities, politics, and laws, were shaped by this idea of the collective, or community. The beginning of intersectionality, as stated in *Race, Class, Gender: Intersections and Inequalities* by Margaret L. Andersen and Patricia Hill Collins Tenth Edition Page 4 is "The fact that race, class, and gender shape the experience of all people in the United States is widely documented in research and to some extent, commonly understood. For years, social scientists have studied the consequences of race, class, and gender as separate forms of inequality for different groups in society. In the United States, race, class, and gender constitute fundamental systems of inequality and, as a result, we know a lot about them individually. The framework of race, class and gender studies presented here, however, explores how race, class, and gender operate together in people's lives. Fundamentally, race, class and gender are intersecting categories of experience that affect all aspects of human life; they simultaneously structure the experience of all people in this society. At any moment, race, class, or gender may feel more salient or meaningful in a given person's life, but they are overlapping and cumulative in their effects."

In the 1800s, this idea came to a head as Charles Darwin postulated that mankind is a new species who emerge from a cycle known as natural selection. This is generally understood by the evolutionary tenets that all species are related to one another through descent, and generational changes are caused by the survival and reproduction of certain advantageous genetic variants. The offspring of those with these advantageous variants survive rather than those without, especially when faced with problems like overpopulation and food shortages. All behaviors can be deduced through these means of survival and reproduction. The idea at that time in history occurred shortly after The Age of Enlightenment, which created a ripe environment for the then well conditioned human community to accept new societal norms. It was concluded, we are all animals at different levels of our development. This idea shaped and formed societies from then, to our present age. The same idea is just packaged differently.

Presently, the term intersectionality is used to incorporate all communities, as the world comes under one collective consciousness. Some of these communities are known as churches, mosques, synagogues, temples, fraternities, sororities, civil rights organizations, lgbtq groups, women's rights groups, black lives matter groups, marriage equality advocates and human rights groups.

C.S Lewis saw this development at the end of the 1900s. As he stated in *The Abolition of Man* pg. 37, "But the man-molders of the new age will be armed with the powers of an omnicompetent state and an irresistible scientific technique: We shall get at last a race of conditioners who really can cut out all posterity in what shape they please."

The word and meaning of a human came about at the end of the primitive world by Greek thinkers and was encapsulated by the philosophers of the enlightenment. We define a human as: a person that thinks with their feelings and desires; no intellect or intelligence to will their actions. The first time the word human is translated from the Hebrew to English or the then recognized language of the day is in Genesis 6:4; the word enosh אנוש is translated as people or human. It carries the meaning to "cause weakness" or, "be frail".

The word human was not known to the Hebrew culture; persons were known as individuals. Persons are to be responsible for their own lives, as they were instructed by the priest about their origin and dependence. Dependence then and now is not on any man, community, or society, but on the person who created all things, Yeshua, Elohim, Yahwheh - ישוה אלוהים יהוה.

In the previous chapter we looked at The Adam as he was made in Elohim's image and likeness. Here, we are going to look at the "likeness" of the man, Adam, as relating to the human as an animal. In Genesis 1:26, the scripture tells us that The Adam was an inanimate lifeless object, until Elohim, Yahweh, formed the dust in His image and likeness. Genesis 1:26: בצלמנו כדמותנו in our image after our likeness.

The persons are being formed, first by the dust - עפר - eapher, which is from the אדמה - adama, meaning earth. The Hebrew word likeness is damoth - דמות, which is also from the adama.

The Hebrew word damoth is a very interesting word that is filled with potentiality. Some meanings of the word can be seen or understood from the parent root, dam - דם, meaning blood. This word has a variety of baby root meanings, e.g., bleeding, hemorrhage, blood flow, sanguineous. Another parent root that can be observed is מת – mut, meaning death. Most words from the Hebrew perspective that relate with killing, dying, and dead, follow this root. The word damam – דמם, from a baby root, means to be silent, bring to a standstill, still, to stop, or to be struck dumb, inanimate.

"For by him were all things created, that are in heaven, and all that are in the earth visible and invisible, whether they be thrones, or dominions, or principalities, or powers, all things were created by him and for him, and he is before all things, and by him all things exist." Colossians 1:16-17.

In Genesis 1:26 Elohim, Jesus - ישוע is making the man like himself. Information is becoming what it is. The first thing to be, is the Word, John 1:1 "In the beginning was the Word and the Word was with God and the Word was God." The Word is information in itself, and the thing that was chosen to decipher the information in all things was the dust - עפר - eapher. This lifeless object, the dust or earth, is now being filled with an intangible, non relational, non substantive, independent life, which we call the soul, the mind, or the spirit. These three words are used interchangeably to refer to the mind, which is the intangible point of reference that relates to the physical brain and nervous system. The flesh cannot be what it is apart from the soul, and vice versa.

In Genesis 2:7, the three persons of the Tri-unity, the Oneness of Elohim אלוהים האחדות is revealed, "The Lord God formed man from the dust of earth, he blew into his nostrils the breath of life and man became a living being". The breath that Elohim blew is the neshama - נשם. "Neshama" means to move air into the man, causing the man to become a living being/soul. The information is now placed in the inanimate object. The object is now informed of what and who it is.

The soul - נפש - nephesh, means rest, return to spiritual repose. It is the reminder to the Adam - אדם of his nature, being tripartite and not dualistic. The soul, which cannot be seen nor understood apart from the flesh and the mind, has been rejected by The Human in today's society.

The flesh - בשר - basar, means to cover with sensitive coating, and the mind - מוח - muach, means to fatten or feel well. This flesh and mind has become the tyrant that says, "we do not have any need for Elohim" because of the information they now have concerning nature, and the things they say formed all other things.

The likeness, damoth – דמות, is literally saying to the now existing living person, the dead lifeless dust is coming to life through the breath of the Creator.

The dust that was not alive is now able to decode the information in itself and other existing things that you can see, taste, touch, smell, and hear. The soul is reminding the mind, the only way you can understand the nature of your being is to listen to the information that has been given to man through the written word and through the moral and ethical aspect of their being in creation; otherwise, they can become animals.

The Adam - אדמ was created male and female as stated in Genesis 1:27.

Male - זכר - zacar, means to store in memory and remember and female - נקבה - nekavah, means hole, perforation, body opening and set firmly.

The male and female are now a reality of The Adam. The unity of The Adam is now made tangible in a dualistic state. The combined meaning of male and female is saying to The Adam (the Unit), that in order for the line between the spiritual and physical to not be blurred, they must keep the distinction between the flesh and mind, inside and outside, right and wrong, male and female, and love and hate. Because the male and female are now relating to the tangible first, rather than that which can only be known through your nephesh - spirit/soul, the female is now a direct expression of what the male is as a person and the male is a direct reminder of what the female is. The male and the female are not greater, bigger, or better than the other, they are both equally one in essence as they were created; however, two expressed in existence. The one, better yet, the two expressed in reality, were to bring glory and worship to their Creator without the mixture of their imagination with the word of another or themselves. Now, the fall has happened and the male and female are in a state of confusion.

Remember, before the female was brought to the male, he was sent to name the animals. In Genesis, Elohim Yahweh said, it is not good that the man be alone, I will make for him a help meet.

Let us take a look at the meaning of the words help - עזר - aezor, which means assistance, i.e., wife and meet - כנגדו - kengedor. The word kengedor is conjugated from two roots, כן - ken - meaning truthful, right, honest, sincere, base, stand, pedestal, and גדד - geda - meaning to cut; concentrate penetration. Before the fall of The Adam, the male ought to have been the reminder that in order to function and operate in accordance with design, he needs to be in constant communication with his bride, just as he had constant communication with his Creator before the female was brought to him.

As the man named all the animals and things that were in his presence, he used the whole essence of his being to relate to the animals; this was his mind, intellect, intelligence, will, and emotions.

Genesis 1:31, "And Elohim saw all that he had made and found it very good".

Up until that time, the male, Adam, operated as a functional person in accordance with his design. While in Genesis 2:20, The Elohim expressed "but for Adam no fitting helper was found." The Adam viewed all the animals as they were, which are non-rational beings. They were not compatible intellectually and emotionally. He viewed their anatomy and came to the conclusion that none of the created animals were able to meet his needs as a person, and he was not able to give the needs of a person to any of the animals.

Adam is now showing the ability to distinguish between conscious being and living being. The female and male were combined as one while The Adam named all the animals. The Adam is showing to all conscious beings that once you are yoked to your bride, no other created being can satisfy what a conscious being can. The Adam is also showing us we have the capacity to become an animal if we choose, but once we are whole, we will not choose to become one. The Adam was made from the dust - עפר - eafar. The dust is responsible for sustaining all plant and animal life. All that the dust receives from nature, it consumes. It then gives the first fruit of all that has been received and consumed to the consumer. The dust is now filled with the spirit, or consciousness of its state. The man is now able to separate his feelings and emotions, which are all physically and biologically stimulated by the outside, apart from the information of Truth "spirit", which is either objective reality or that which he chooses to follow.

The Adam now leads his life as he knows it ought to be. The essence of all physical men is found in the Hebrew word, eafar:

ע – ayin, the man who sees and understands
פ – pey, the mouth which speaks the truth.
ר – resh, the head which follows the true leader.

An example of this essence is found in Matthew 10:1-10 and John 5:1-47.

The male Adam is now given his compatible part, or whole, his female Adam. The male and female are The Adam; they are whole. The female Adam saw the fruit to be desirable to make her wise, as stated in Genesis 3:6. They took the fruit and mixed it with their imagination. The moment they mixed the fruit with what they imagined; a shift took place in their minds.

The process of their thinking was then reversed. The Adam is a person who was created to think from their intellect, intelligence, will, and emotions. From the moment they ate the fruit of the tree of knowledge of good and evil, they became the animals we now know as humans. A human thinks from their feelings, emotions, will, intellect, and then intelligence. The 'eafar' is now viewed from an entirely physical perspective, instead of leading to The Adam's Creator. The flesh is viewed as the only hope for mankind. The Adam wants to be covered with earthly substances only as a result of the fall. The first time we see the word human translated in the scripture is in Genesis 6:4. The word אנש - enosh - meaning to cause weakness or be frail, gave rise to the human coming into existence as a result of the physical appeal. It is not that physical or emotional desires are wrong, but when the intellect is directed as a result of the eyes and the imagination, which are the emotions, a new being arises, the human. This being, the human, is dysfunctional and sinful. The humans pass the blame or responsibility to another, and always rely on another for direction. This state of reliance and blame on man is as a result of the fall of The Adam. The state the man now finds himself in has been echoed by the giving of the Torah, which is known as the Chamash or the first five books of the bible, The Law. The humans showed themselves throughout the years, culminating at the beginning of the A.D era, that they are incapable of keeping the sayings or instructions of Yahweh. Humans keep creating new laws and kingdoms that will justify their desires and actions.

The human's fallen state is at its zenith when they choose not to recognize the truth for what it is in reality. Around AD 33, at the trial of Yeshua, Pontius Pilate asked Yeshua the question, "What is truth?" John 18:38.

The question, "what is truth?" rose to a crescendo at that time in history when The Word of Scripture and the experience of Israel's past, came face to face with the manifestation of The Word of Scripture, Yeshua, and their experience. This question was asked before by Jacob and Moses in a different way.

Jacob said, "Please tell me your name." Genesis 32:29.

Moses asked Elohim, "If I go to the Israelites and say to them: The God of your fathers has sent me to you, and they ask me, 'What is His name?' what should I tell them?"

Exodus 3:13

Today the same question is phrased in many different ways. Here are a few:

1. What is real?
2. Can you prove you exist?
3. How can you know anything is what you claim it to be?
4. How can you know the Bible is the Truth?
5. Can you know the Truth?

Some people resort to thinking, the only truth there is, is scientific truth. All fallen men ask the question about truth as a result of their identity and the invisibility of reality.

The question Pilate asked Yeshua about his kingdom and his kingship had to do with the invisibility of his knowledge. The knowledge Pilate had accumulated concerning the forms and the abstract, were now being viewed through the prism of Yeshua's silence and his few words. All that was taught by Plato concerning the forms are now bearing correspondence with Yeshua's person.

Historical events are important in understanding reality in relation to eternity.

Pilate was the fifth governor of the Roman province, Judea, from 26/27 to 36/37 CE under Tiberius the Emperor. He is best remembered as the official who presided over the trial of Yeshua. Pilate, being trained in Grecian culture and philosophy, knew of the teachings of Plato and Aristotle. Plato thought that the ultimate form was an impersonal force called the good. All men possess an a priori knowledge of reality and can determine and distinguish right from wrong.

"So, when the Gentiles, who do not have the law, instinctively do what the law demands, they are a law to themselves even though they do not have the law. They show that the work of the law is written on their hearts. Their consciences testify in support of this and their competing thoughts either accuse or excuse them." Romans 2:14-15.

Aristotle, a student of Plato held an opposing view of reality and was conducive in establishing materialistic ideologies through his argument which states, all that exists is matter and man was born without knowing right from wrong; this is known as tabula rasa. By studying, investigating, and teaching, man can and will acquire knowledge.

"Remind them of these things, charging them before Elohim not to fight about words; this is in no way profitable and leads to the ruin of the hearers. Be diligent to present yourself approved to Elohim, a worker who does not need to be ashamed, correctly teaching the word of truth. 2 Timothy 2:14-15.

Pilate is now confronted with the invisible Truth and the material object of the Truth, Yeshua. He, Yeshua, is the dabar/logos/word, and the basar/sarx/flesh.

Pilate utilized the information that was taught by Plato and Aristotle. The truth of a thing can be known by the mere existence of that thing. The truth is what it is.

Pilate used his reasoning, together with the information he had and is now receiving about Yeshua and found it to be plausible. After further examination with Yeshua, Pilate went outside again and said to them "Look, I'm bringing Him outside to you to let you know I find no grounds for charging Him." John 19:4

Pilate, with his philosophy and acquired knowledge of Yeshua, gave a subjective response to the charges that were brought before him concerning Yeshua. The ideas that reigned in his mind evoked a response that was true to himself. The person of Yeshua corresponded to Pilate's reasoning and information of reality.

Before we go further, we need to define some terms:

1. Truth bearer: A truth bearer is a person that possesses the knowledge of a thing that exists apart from the awareness of another.

2. Truth maker: A truth maker is the thing that is visible or invisible, physically present, to another person.

3. A witness: Attestation of a fact or event. A witness is one that gives evidence and who has personal knowledge of something.

Pilate, together with his statement about Yeshua, proved that Yeshua makes the truth of reality what it is, in relation to his physical person. Put another way, the information that Pilate had about Yeshua corresponded with what Yeshua is presently before him. However, there was no person, visibly or invisibly present, to corroborate his statement that Yeshua is innocent. There was no witness. At that moment, Yeshua became the Truth maker to Pilate's subjective statement.

The Jews knew of their experience with the Word of Elohim. It was first given to them by Moses, then displayed through the acts performed by the Prophets, as they carried it with them during their sojourn. The Jews corporately had an experiential, pragmatic, and working knowledge with the Tanakh. They knew it to be true based on their experience. However, they rejected the manifestation of the Tanakh, Yeshua, due to them not having another witness to corroborate Yeshua's claim. The Jews, as a corporate unit, were the witnesses necessary to put Yeshua to death. The Pharisees were the voice of the masses, and the people repeated what they said.

"The one condemned to die is to be executed on the testimony of two or three witnesses. No one is to be executed on the testimony of a single witness." Deuteronomy 17:6.

By rejecting the truth of reality for what it is and choosing not to view the past based on historically factual events, a human can harden their emotions and feelings to the point where the intellect can not be reached with the facts. The human now allows its reasoning or intelligence to be guided by their emotions and feelings, "speaking lies in hypocrisy; having their conscience seared with a hot iron" 1 Timothy 4:2.

1. What is Truth?
2. What is a Human?
3. What is a Person?
4. Who am I?

These questions which are revisited by all men throughout time, past and present, can be seen and understood in the death of Yeshua on Calvary as stated in Matthew 27:38.

The act of Yeshua, as he hung between the two thieves on the cross, reestablished the Person's will once again. Metaphorically speaking, the three men who are placed on the crosses as a result of their crimes, represents the one individual human who at all times, has a choice. The three men represent the conscience of a human. The first thief represents the emotions and feelings while the second thief represents the intellect and intelligence; Yeshua represents the will of the human.

In the garden of Eden, the Person died, and the Human came alive. On the cross the Human died, and the Person is rebirthed. The thief that recognized his dysfunctionality and accepted the truth for what it is, being a sinner unable to keep the law even with the help of the rabbis and unable to listen to Yahweh, accepted Yeshua Hamashiach (Jesus the Christ) as the promised seed, for fallen man's reconciliation. This thief metaphorically represents the mind, intellect, intelligence, will, and emotions of all thinking humans who accept the finished acts of Yeshua.

"For just as through one man's disobedience the many were made sinners, so also through the one man's obedience the many will be made righteous." Romans 5:19

The other thief represents the human who continues to reject the truth for what it is. He allows what he thinks, based on what he feels and wants, to direct his words, as he said, "save us and save yourself if you are the Mashiach" Luke 23:39

These three men that were crucified on Calvary, represent the Adam as a corporate solidarity of human's nature as they became after the fall. The thief that said, "save yourself and us", represents the emotions of a human, while the other thief who repented, represents a human who allows himself to be touched by the presence of Yeshua and willingly respond to his conscience. The call for a relationship was made by the two thieves. The thief, who said "remember me", needed a relationship with the truth as a result of reason and truth. This thief made his decision on the known future, not on the tried past.

The other thief called out for a relationship too. This relationship was based on the tried past which he was familiar with. Basing his request on his emotions and feelings, he accepted his will, rather than the given will, which was right beside him.

The known future is the Promised Seed, Yeshua, while the tried past is the fruit of religion and man's attempt to reach HaShem.

The conscience is the free willed Person who can be directed by the intellect or the emotions. The thief who said, "remember me", is the Person who chooses the seed, Yeshua. The thief who chose this life is the Human who chooses to remember the opportunities he had and will keep remembering each event for ever and ever separated from Yeshua, which is death. Yeshua said, "come to me and learn of me, I am life eternal."

The thief who said remember me, is showing to all men then and now, it is only when they are ready to die to themselves, intellectually and emotionally, that their consciousness/spirit/soul is touched by the Mashiach and they begin to live. Yeshua represents the Spirit of men as he hangs between the two thieves. He is always there to quicken the spirit, soul, and consciousness of the human who asks for that relationship.

Who are you going to listen to?

Are you going to listen to your intellect, emotions, or spirit, apart from Him or allow yourself to be quickened by the crucified and risen Yeshua?

Humans are societally manufactured and reproduced while Persons are doctrinally positioned in the Love, Truth, and Goodness of Mashiach.

A visible person is limited to their humanity; however, a human is not limited to their humanity. They can become animals and beyond. See behavioral chart characteristics.

After a person uses their mind, they can experience and understand the behavior of a human and an animal.

	HUMAN	PERSON	ANIMAL
	Brain/Mind	Brain/Mind	Brain/Mind
	Feel	Think	Feel
	Instinctive	Know	Instinctive
	React	Intelligent	React
	Create	Reproduce	Reproduce
	Prefer	Need	Need
	Play	Experience	Play
	Accept	Question	Accept
	Happy/Fun	Joy	Happy/Fun
	Destructive	Peaceful	Destructive
	Demand	Relational	Demand
	Attack	Respond	Attack

גוּף – Body
בשר – Flesh
עור - Skin

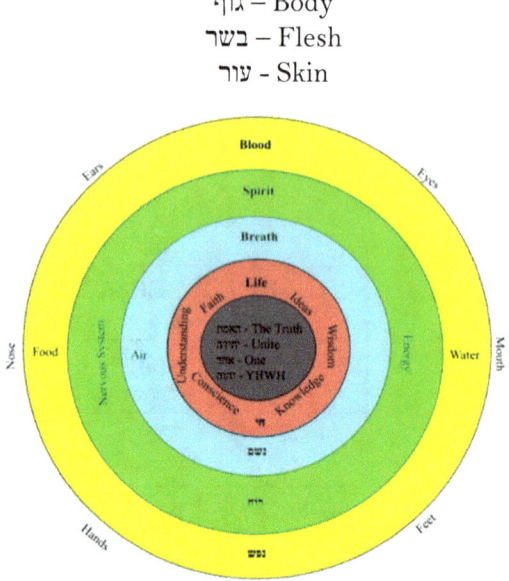

This diagram of The Seed - הזרע depicts the process of how man goes from living, to having a relationship with Yeshua eternally. The seed, which represents the continuation of the human species, was threatened from the time the man abrogated his responsibility and allowed the woman to provide the means for food, through an economic system that was prohibited by Elohim. Genesis 2:16-17

The Seed which was provided to the man by Elohim for the reproduction of his offspring is now corrupt as a result of the woman being allowed to provide food for the family through a distortion of their anthropological nature. The Adam was designed to provide safety and food for himself and his wife's physical life. He, however, provided death as a result of his focus on self.

All what the Creator made was good, even the flesh, yet the seed became corrupt. The Elohim then set in motion the reestablishment of the family. The man being the provider for life, having the seed, which is known as the sperm, is no longer reliable as pure. He disabled his reproductive prowess by relinquishing responsibility to his female.

After envisioning the fruit (Genesis 3:6) to be desirable for obtaining wisdom and then eating thereof, the Adam acquired knowledge of their nakedness and solidified their choice by sewing loincloths with fig leaves for themselves. Rejecting their designed covering for a false version of reality conjured by their imagination and the word of another, they inadequately tried to cover up, signifying their new state of separation from Elohim. The relationship that was once had with their Creator has now been obstructed by a barrier made by themselves. They allowed their experience to dictate their morality rather than following the prescribed path by their Creator. With their eyes now opened to a fallen, disconnected reality, the Adam was confronted by Elohim and went into hiding. When found, they presented themselves in a state of fear due to their nakedness, reflecting their knowledge of the new barrier between them and Elohim. As a result, the Elohim provided a covering made of skins for Adam and his wife, as a sign of remembrance and shame of their choice to separate from their Creator; this marks the redemptive process of Elohim.

The woman who willingly received from her surroundings by eating the fruit, is now given the choice to receive the seed of Elohim through His way of redemption. This act of acceptance came with the price of her body, spirit, breath, and life; the sacrifice known as childbearing and birth marks the entry of The Messiah.

"I will put hostility between you and the woman, and between your seed and her seed. He will strike your head, and you will strike his heel." Genesis 3:15

The woman received the seed willingly.

> "Then the angel told her: Do not be afraid, Mary, for you have found favor with Elohim. Now listen: you will conceive and give birth to a son, and you will call His name Yeshua…"I am the Lord's slave," said Mary. "May it be done to me according to your word." Then the angel left her." Luke 1:30-31, 38.

Mary, having an understanding of The Scriptures, knew what the prophet Isaiah spoke concerning the coming Saviour, who is necessary for the life that mankind was called to live before the fall. Mary exclaimed to Elohim.

"My soul proclaims the greatness of the Lord, and my spirit has rejoiced in Elohim my Saviour… "He has satisfied the hungry with good things and sent the rich away empty." Luke 1:46, 55.

Mary now represents the fulfillment of the prophecy spoken by Elohim in Genesis 3:15, repeated by the Prophet Isaiah (7:14; 9:6-7) and made known to mankind in John 1:12.

The roles of the man and woman appear to be reversed as the woman is providing the seed for all of mankind's provision and safety, and the man is receiving what the woman has provided as the necessary water, bread, and food for eternal life.

The order of function for the family has been corrected as the woman accepted her role as an eazor-kengedor, as echoed by Paul in his letter to Timothy. (1 Timothy 2:8-15)

"And Adam was not deceived, but the woman was deceived and transgressed. But she will be saved through childbearing, if she continues in faith, love, and holiness, with good sense." (vv. 14-15)

At the beginning of the first century, the concept of a woman giving birth to a son without the aid of a man was looked upon as superstition. We are now living at a time where the very idea of a thing can be materialized on the basis of the producer's choice.

Technology is increasing at rapid speed. Man can make whatever kind of human they desire: man, woman, and anything in between along with varying phenotypes. Mankind is now manipulating the very genes of the cell. Whatever a human desires, they can request it from their provider/creator, the scientist.

Scientists can only manipulate the life after the egg and the sperm fuse together (fertilization). This fertilization results in a diploid cell, also known as a zygote שליל - sheleel. Before the fusion of the two cells, the scientists do not know what the person will begin to exist as, either a male or female. These scientists can only view the chromosomes and alter the deoxyribonucleic acid (DNA) according to the requests from the buyer, or their own agenda.

THE FAMILY - המשפחה

Based on the Random House Unabridged dictionary, a family is described as a "basic social unit consisting of parents and their children, considered as a group, whether dwelling together or not". The traditional family is a fundamental group in any society.

The definition as it were, or the original meaning of the word has been preserved through the ages. The word family from the Hebrew is משפחה - mishpachah - a family, circle of relatives, a class of persons, a species of animals or sort of things, a tribe, or people (Strongs Concordance pg. 98).

The Bible discloses a family to be a Husband and Wife.

Yahweh, after making all things, spirit, and human, both the spirits and humans, visible and invisible, devolved. The spirits devolved to a non-redeemable state, while humans devolved into an animalistic state. However, according to Scripture, the state of humanity is redeemable.

The Adam persons devolved to a state of humanity where they formed groups and nations by which they created their own identity. Yahweh, knowing the nature of fallen man, established the family as it is the final state for man's redemption. Isaiah 46:10

A person in their human state can no longer hear the voice or spirit of Elohim calling and directing them from the inside–that is their mind, intellect, intelligence, will, emotions and feelings–as a result of the mixture of their imagination with reality. They are unable to identify truth. Man is never able to know truth apart from the direction of the Word of Elohim, they can only know truth in relation to contingency.

The Hebrew word Mishpachah is a compound word. It consists of the words: משפט – Mishpat, meaning trial, judgement, and law and פחה – Phachah, meaning to govern, and rule local areas. This word, Mishpachah, shows and reflects the responsibility of the father in the home. As we are all very familiar with the saying "Charity begins at home and ends abroad" the definition of the word charity/love, is to give what belongs to the other or to give what is not yours. The man, (male and female) is not able to discern their purpose for being, independent of the other. Man, only sees things as it relates to themselves, naturally.

Yahweh in His wisdom, placed on the male and female person the substance of their desire and the nature of their persons, which serves as the expression of what love is and as a reminder of the image of Elohim being expressed on their persons as the family.

This reminder that was placed on the man is his name biologically; from the Hebrew, זכר - Zacar, meaning to remember, recall, maleness, penis, and on the woman, with her biological name being נקבה – Nekavah - which means hole, aperture, tunnel, woman, female, and feminine. These names no longer serve as the truth maker for either the man or the woman.

The new nature of the Adam (male and female) is unable to be identified from the inside. This is because of the mixture of the fruit, imagination, and reality, which is sin. The mind of both the man and the woman became corrupted and they were not able to see or understand the whole picture of reality, objective truth.

The reminder for The Adam was before them, however, they were unable to correspond it with the nature of their whole state of being, which is physical and spiritual. Remember, The Adam is one that became two physical beings, having one spiritual dependence. In order to know the truth, there must be two things that correspond to the thing that is now claiming to be what it is. There must also be an independent individual that justifies the claim. For The Adam to be what they are as a unit, there must be three persons. The male – זכר corresponds with the female – נקבה in the physical sense, as their physical bodies correspond to the Hebrew Scriptures and what The Spirit of The Word – דבר says that the man and the woman is. Genesis 2:21-24, 1 Corinthians 7:4, Ephesians 5:25-29.

The man and woman cannot continue existence apart from knowing themselves as One; being sexually whole, as the scripture says. When the principle of Husband and Wife is followed on the basics of nature, the relationship of a necessary being is realized. Hebrews 13:4

Marriage is honourable in all, and the bed undefiled. This is the objective moral value that corresponds to the invisible being that is revealed through general observation and by special revelation as disclosed in the scripture.

From a biological perspective, The Adam can know that they are One when they reproduce a child. The child is independent of the Husband and Wife, yet dependent on the two to become one as a person, while The Spirit gives life to the sperm and egg resulting in an individual child.

The image of Elohim (tsalem – צלם) can now be seen through the relationship of the Husband and Wife as they are directed by their Creator, The Spirit of The Word.

Genesis 1:26 "And God said, Let Us make man in our image, after our likeness: and let them have dominion 1:27 So God created man in His own image, in the image of God created he him; male and female created he them. 2:7 And the LORD God formed man of the dust of the ground, and breathed into his nostrils the breath of life; and man became a living soul. 2:21-23 And the LORD God caused a deep sleep to fall upon Adam, and he slept: and he took one of the ribs, and closed up the flesh instead thereof; And the rib which the LORD God had taken from man, made he a woman, and brought her unto the man. And Adam said, This is now bone of my bones and flesh of my flesh: she shall be called Woman because she was taken out of Man."

After the Lord brought the woman to the man, he expressed his individuality as a whole unit with his wife. He expressed the true nature of his being as dependent on the breath of life, which is Elohim's Word.

Genesis 2:24 "Therefore shall a man leave his father and his mother and shall cleave unto his wife, and they shall be one flesh." Adam is saying to us families, you cannot know The Creator apart from embracing your true nature as a male and female unit. This forms the Oneness of the being of man that is now dependent on the Spirit, Breath, and Word of Elohim, which is good.

In functioning as a Good unit, which is in accordance with design, the essence of love is expressed; this happens through the giving and receiving of what does and does not belong to you, as expressed by Yahweh through Yeshua. This is now visible for the family to see and to act accordingly, as the husband dies from all sexual needs and desires from other human and animal attractions, intellectually and physically.

The man is showing to all created human beings that they ought not to function in accordance with their human genus, which is aligned to the animal kingdom housed within nature. The man is showing to all humans, rather than appeal to only the physical that is readily available, he must incorporate the whole man, the intangible, non-visible nature to determine what is right from wrong, good from bad, and love from hate.

The non-visible intangible nature of the human is known as the Person. As we said earlier, a person is one that possesses a mind, will, intellect, intelligence, and emotions. We see before the fall of The Human; the male person was using the whole aspect of his personhood to dispel all animalistic behavior. As stated in Genesis 2:23 "And Adam said this time bone from my bone", it suggests that he looked at all that was created, before the woman was brought forth. The male person made a mindful decision that incorporated his intellect, intelligence, will, and then emotions, in that order, when he exclaimed "bone of my bone and flesh of my flesh". The emotion within this encapsulates all what the mind knows, reasons, and pursues, as justified true belief, which is neutral.

The conclusion of the whole matter of man's identity is this: what he loves or hates rests on his mind. The mind is the element, part, substance, or the process that reasons, thinks, feels, wills, perceives, and judges; that which is in oneself or other conscious beings. This is known in Hebrew as the dah - דעה.

In the mind houses these four processes:

1. Sakal שכל: Intellect - The power or faculty of the mind by which one knows or understands, as distinguished from that which one feels and wills; the faculty of thinking and acquiring knowledge.

2. Binah בינה: Intelligence - The capacity for learning, reasoning, understanding, and similar forms of mental activities; aptitude in grasping truths, relationships, facts, meanings, etc.

3. Rots רוץ: Will - am about or going to; to run.

4. Regosh ריגוש: Emotion - An affective state of consciousness in which joy, sorrow, fear, hate, or the likes is experienced as distinguished from a cognitive and volitional state of consciousness.

As we put this sequence of two thoughts together, we can come to the conclusion that only a person can know Yeshua HaMashiach, Jesus the Christ. A human can not know the Christ apart from utilizing their mind, which will bring them to the understanding of a person. A person can then confess with their mouth and accept the stated words of Yeshua, that they are sick, broken, and dysfunctional, in need of help.

If you say, "have mercy on me, a willing law breaker, only you can fix my soul and give me access to the tree of life eternal", Yeshua will open the door of life to you as you first open your door of death to his living Word.

Romans 10:8-11

If you did that, I want to be the first to say welcome to the reason, and the truth to believe with your mind, that Yeshua HaMashiach is the risen savior of all mankind, and is the head of His body and husband to His bride. Continue to fight, the battle has been won; you are now a man of Elohim.

www.ingramcontent.com/pod-product-compliance
Lightning Source LLC
LaVergne TN
LVHW020416070526
838199LV00054B/3629